The story of
Santa Claus

The story of
Santa Claus

TERESA CHRIS

CHARTWELL
BOOKS, INC.

A QUINTET BOOK

Published by Chartwell Books
A Division of Book Sales, Inc.
110 Enterprise Avenue
Secaucus, New Jersey 07094

ISBN 1-55521-782-6

Reprinted 1993

This book was designed and produced by
Quintet Publishing Limited
6 Blundell Street
London N7 9BH

Creative Director: Richard Dewing
Designer: Peter Laws
Project Editor: William Hemsley
Editor: Sam Merrell
Picture Researcher: Jill-Anne De Cet

Typeset in Great Britain by
Central Southern Typesetters, Eastbourne
Manufactured in Singapore by
Bright Arts (Singpore) Pte Ltd
Printed in Singapore by
Star Standard Industries Pte Ltd

CONTENTS

PREFACE

There seems a magic in the very name of Christmas.
CHARLES DICKENS

'Twas the week before Christmas and I had just spent several frustrating hours in the San Francisco Public Library, trying to complete research for this book. Desperately in need of tea, I headed out through the security gates into the late, cool, grey afternoon. The Polk bus home had just drawn up. Relieved that at least something had gone right I joined the queue and stepped aboard.

In one of the front seats sat the best personification of Santa Claus I have ever seen. He was perfect; from head to toe no detail could be faulted. His girth was round, and his locks were curled and silvery-white. On rosy, round cheeks balanced a pair of gold-rimmed glasses. A black belt encircled the traditional red suit. So perfect was he it seemed rude to stare. This, it appeared, was not one of Santa's "helpers", but Santa Claus himself.

Seated, I watched the reactions of the rest of the passengers as they boarded. On came a young boy, about five years old, a Bill Cosby look-alike helped forward by his father. Clutching a box of animal crackers, he moved down the bus until he saw Santa and his father suggested he take the empty seat next to the well-known gentleman. Suddenly the child's body went rigid, and with eyes big, hands frozen around the box of cookies he marched forward like an automaton. Obediently he settled next to Santa, dwarfed by the adult-sized plastic seat. Santa Claus put his arm around him in a protective manner and questioned the child about what he wanted for Christmas. Had he been a good boy? What had he received last year? Santa stressed that he would try to bring the boy what he wanted, but in case he could not the boy must remember that Santa loved him, his parents loved him and most of all God loved him. Santa put the child at ease and encouraged him to answer, and was so much my own image of Santa that tears came to my eyes. The little boy was not the only one affected by the figure. We were all watching the power of Santa Claus.

Eventually it was time for the child and his father to get off. Still in a daze the boy was encouraged to thank Santa and

LEFT
The jolly bearded face of Santa Claus with his red, fur-trimmed hat and coat must be one of the most easily recognized and best loved images in the world.

RIGHT
Santa Claus with children in an old Christmas card. More than anyone children love Santa, and perhaps Santa loves children best of all.

ABOVE
Santa asks a young child what she would like for Christmas, his bulging sack of presents on the floor behind him.

LEFT

Some cherubs seem to have decided to help Santa carry the presents, but they can carry little when compared to Santa's sack.

RIGHT

Not two Santas, but two Raphael Tuck relief prints of Santa Claus, still joined together.

say goodbye. The spectacle was almost over, but not quite. I was fascinated to watch the reactions of the adults as they got on the bus. Respectfully they greeted Santa. The man now seated next to him responded seriously to Santa's questions about what he had been doing that day. A lady called from the back of the bus and asked Santa Claus what he was going to do about the recession.

There were none of the questions or jokes one might expect. There was not even a trace of facetiousness in their attitudes, or any sign that they were just playing along. Everyone remembered Santa in their own childhood. Santa Claus was in our midst. Santa Claus had come to town!

CHAPTER ONE

INTRODUCTION

The nights draw in and there is a tingle in the air. Advent calendars are hung and with each window opened Christmas draws tantalizingly nearer. Everywhere are signs of the coming festivities.

The streets of town centres are transformed by coloured lights, strung from side to side. They are shaped into bells, stars or other symbols associated with the season. So spectacular are some of these displays that a trip "to see the lights" has become a seasonal tradition in many places. Lamp-posts are garlanded with greenery – the traditional holly, ivy and boughs of pine. Shops boast gaily decorated windows, with themes ranging from simple red and green to complete Christmas trees. The department stores all try to outdo each other in the complexity and sumptuousness of their decorations and tableaux. Fully animated scenes from such favourites as *The Christmas Carol* or "The Twelve Days of Christmas" stretch from window to window. Passers-by gather outside and children are pushed to the front of the crowd, all eager to see

better. Some stores have even arranged formal queues, confident that their display will not just attract a quick curious glance. Eyes widen at the extravagance and the cleverness. Children stare, spellbound by the tricks being performed and the magic of another Christmas.

The air is full of the sound of carols coming from the shop doorways, blending with the singing of the Salvation Army and the tinkling of their bells as they collect money for the poor. People's breath makes white puffs in the cold air, as they hurry from place to place. Chestnuts are roasted on street corners by men wearing half-mitten gloves.

The shops are warm and heavy with the smell of pine needles and cones. Streamers are festooned overhead and displays are dusted with silver frosting or puffy cotton snow. Shoppers bustle and jostle each other. Everywhere there is the excitement of gift buying. Tills ring busily as the biggest shopping season of the year gets underway. Deep in the heart of the larger stores or malls, Santa Claus can be found in his "Grotto"

LEFT
Gathering candles, wreaths of dark foliage and flowers, holly with bright berries, shining silver and a host of other decorations is part of the preparation for Christmas.

RIGHT AND
BELOW
*Restaurants, shops,
malls and other
trading places all
decorate their premises
as part of the
festivities, much to the
delight of passing
Christmas shoppers.*

LEFT AND RIGHT
Snow, trees and bright lights can give a whole town the feel of Christmas. And when there is snow during the festive season, what could be more fun that building not just one but a whole family of snow people.

or "Toyland" – the highlight of any child's shopping expedition. Mixed with excitement are fear and wonder at the big man with his strange red suit and hood trimmed with white fur, his black belt and big boots. Most imposing of all are his long, white, curling beard and whiskers, which tickle your face as you try and tell him you have been a good girl or boy and what you would most like for Christmas. The countdown of the number of shopping days to go till Christmas is announced on television and radio and in the newspapers.

FESTIVE PREPARATIONS

At home families spend weeks getting ready for the celebration. The houses are decorated inside and out. Fairy lights are hung in trees and looped around bushes or even around the whole house. Some homes glow with plain white lights, others with red and green or a colourful mixture, twinkling on and off. Each display shares with the others in proclaiming the joy of the season. Wandering around a neighbourhood you can see not only simple strings of lights, but also illuminated models of

RIGHT
Decorating the Christmas tree can be an activity for the whole family. Here three generations help each other with the pleasurable task.

LEFT
Hanging up the mistletoe is an old Christmas custom, here lampooned in an magazine illustration from around 1900.

the favourite Christmas figures. A nativity scene in one garden, a snowman in another and, perhaps most impressive of all, Santa Claus in his sleigh being pulled across the roof of a house by his reindeer.

There is the excitement of bringing home the Christmas tree, and decorating it with the precious ornaments collected over the years and often passed down from a previous generation. Christmas music may be playing in the background, and eggnog or mulled wine is drunk. Holly, ivy and boughs of pine are garlanded around banisters and looped on mantel-pieces,

with a ball of mistletoe hung strategically in the hall. The house is ready – looking its festive best.

Christmas is especially the time for feasting, and delicious aromas fill the house as Christmas cakes and mince pies are prepared and baked. There is the ritual making of the Christmas pudding, with each member of the family taking turns to stir the mixture and make a wish for the following year. Ordered are the turkey and the ham or whatever food is traditional in the house. Some have the dense Christmas cake, layered with marzipan and thick with white icing resembling

ABOVE

Dark green holly with bright red berries is one of the most traditional symbols of Christmas — and throwing snowballs one of the most traditional activities in the snowy season!

RIGHT

Tucked warm in their beds, children can not stay awake to see Santa arrive, however hard they try, perhaps tired out by all the excitement of Christmas eve.

snow, and decorated with tiny figures on top. Larders and refrigerators are stocked up with food and plenty to drink.

Meanwhile the children are engrossed in the school nativity play or carol concert, the Christmas dinners and parties, and the most important thing of all, writing to Santa Claus to let him know what they want. Adults are busy trying to find odd cupboards and shelves where they can hide presents, away from prying eyes, sometimes so successfully that they are occasionally not found for months or even years afterwards.

Christmas cards are bought or made and sent to relatives, friends and acquaintances, frequently to people who only communicate at this one time of the year. Christmas is seen as a time for reaching out, the sharing of goodwill and the year's worth of news. The postal workers put in long hours to deliver the millions of Christmas cards and gifts.

Schools break up and families come home to be together for the holiday. Carollers go around singing from door to door and "I'm Dreaming of a White Christmas" is nostalgically playing on the radio.

Finally it is Christmas Eve, and the atmosphere is one of thrilled anticipation. For this is the night that everyone has been waiting for. This is the night when Santa Claus will come, bringing gifts that everyone has longed and hoped for. Children are overexcited and loath to go to bed, because they are determined to see Santa riding through the sky or climbing down the chimney. Stockings are hung by the fireplace or at the foot of the bed ready to be filled, and refreshments are laid out for his arrival.

Gradually, however, everyone gets to bed and the house is silent – waiting for Santa Claus.

ABOVE
A Thomas Nast illustration shows a boy testing Santa's generosity by hanging up an enormous stocking.

CHAPTER TWO

THE ORIGIN OF SANTA CLAUS

The easiest thing to explain about the origin of Santa Claus is his name. Santa Claus comes from the Dutch words "Sinter Klaas", which is what they familiarly call their favourite saint, St Nicholas, whose feast day is on the 6 December.

Nicholas lived in what is now called Turkey. He was born in about AD 280 in the town of Patras. His parents were wealthy and he was well-educated. He seems to have had a remarkable childhood. While still a young boy he was made Bishop of Myra, and because of this he has been known ever since as the Boy Bishop. He was renowned for his extreme kindness and generosity – often going out at night and taking presents to the needy. There are many stories about his goodness, his love of children and the miracles he performed. On a voyage to the Holy Land, he was said to have quelled a tempest, and restored life to a dying sailor. There are two stories that are particularly relevant and provide a reason for his becoming Santa Claus.

THE THREE DAUGHTERS

The first story shows his innate generosity. There were three unmarried girls living in Patras who came from a good family, but they could not get married because their father had lost all his money and so they had no dowries. The only thing the father thought he could do was to sell them when they reached marriageable age. Hearing of their imminent fate, Nicholas secretly delivered a bag of gold to the eldest daughter, who was at the right age for marriage but had despaired of ever finding a suitor. Her family was thrilled at her good fortune, and she went on to become happily married. When the next daughter came of age, Nicholas delivered gold to her also.

According to the story handed down, Nicholas threw the bag through the window and it landed in the daughter's stocking, which she had hung by the fire to dry. Another version claims that Nicholas dropped the bag of gold down the chimney.

By the time the youngest daughter was old enough for marriage, the father was determined to discover his daughters'

XXV

ΟΑ.ΝΙΚΟΛΑΟΣ.

BELOW
A Tuck relief print of Santa. There is still some hint of a resemblace between this relatively modern portrayal and the picture to the right.

LEFT
An engraving of St Nicholas as Archbishop

RIGHT

One of the stories of St Nicholas tells how he quelled a storm, thus saving a ship and its sailors. This picture by Albrecht Altdorfer shows St Nicholas blessing the ship's crew while a devilish figure sits on top of the bending mast.

LEFT
St Nicholas climbs up to a window to secretly throw a bag of gold to one of the three daughters. The picture was painted by Lorenzo di Bicci in 1433.

benefactor. He, not unnaturally, thought that she might be given a bag of gold too, so he decided to keep watch all night. Nicholas, true to form, arrived and was seized, and his identity and generosity were made known to all. As similar stories of the bishop's generosity spread, anyone who received an unexpected gift thanked St Nicholas.

ST NICHOLAS AND CHILDREN

Another one of the many stories told about St Nicholas explains why he was made the patron saint of children. On a journey to Nicaea he stopped on the way and put up at an inn. During the night he dreamt that a terrible crime had been committed in the building. His dream was quite horrific. In it three young

sons of a wealthy Asian, on their way to study in Athens, had been murdered and robbed by the innkeeper. The next morning he confronted the innkeeper and forced him to confess. Apparently the innkeeper had previously murdered other guests and salted them down for pork or had dismembered their bodies and pickled them in casks of brine. The three boys were still there in their casks, and Nicholas made the sign of the cross over them and they were restored to life.

His natural affinity with children led Nicholas to be adopted as their patron saint, and his generosity to the custom of giving gifts to them on his feast day. This custom became especially widespread in the Low Countries, where the Dutch seamen had carried reports home of the saint's generosity. St Nicholas

THE STORY OF SANTA CLAUS

RIGHT
St Nicholas restores the three youths who had been murdered and dismembered by the innkeeper to life. This woodcut dates from the Middle Ages.

RIGHT
A stone relief from the Basilica of St Nicholas, Bari, showing St Nicholas surrounded by important events from his life (for example, restoring the murdered youths to life is the second scene from the bottom on the right).

was, however, a tremendously popular saint everywhere. Both Russia and Greece adopted him as their patron saint, and there are more churches in the world named after him than any of the apostles. The Netherlands, for instance, boasts an inordinate number of them.

In the European countries St Nicholas is usually pictured as a bearded saint, wearing ecclesiastical robes and riding a white horse. He carries a basket of gifts for the good children and a bunch of rods for the naughty ones.

In old Czechoslovakia, *Svaty Mikulas* was brought down from heaven on a golden cord by an angel. When he arrived on Christmas Day, the children rushed to the table to say their prayers. If they did well, he told the angel who came with him to give them their presents.

In parts of the Alps, "ghosts of the field" cleared the way for St Nicholas. Behind them came a man wearing a goat's head, and a masked demon with a birch switch. In Germany 12 young men dressed in straw and wearing animal masks danced along after St Nicholas, ringing cowbells. At each house, after gifts were given, the masked men drove the young people out and pretended to beat them!

ST NICHOLAS' DAY

For the children of the Netherlands, 6 December is still more exciting than Christmas Day, for then St Nicholas arrives. His arrival is celebrated and this is the day when children receive their presents. The excitement begins on the last Saturday in November, when everywhere can be heard the words, "Look there is the steamer bringing us St Nick!"

He traditionally arrives by sea and disembarks at Amsterdam. He then mounts a white horse for a processional ride through the streets. He is clothed in a bishop's scarlet cope and mitre, and wears white gloves and an enormous bishop's ring on his left hand. He is accompanied by Black Peter. St Nicholas' arrival is greeted with cheers from the thousands of children and adults who line the route. He has supposedly come from Spain. This story can be traced back to the sixteenth century when the Spanish dominated the Low Countries. The doublet, puffed velvet breeches, hose and plumed beret worn by his attendants – and in particular Black Peter – are another forcible reminder of that period. Black Peter carries a large sack in which he is said to put all the boys and girls who have mis-behaved during the course of the past 12 months. He will carry them all away to Spain.

RIGHT
RIGHT
*St Nicholas arrives in
Amsterdam, having
disembarked from his
ship, dressed in
bishop's robes and
riding on his white
horse.*

BELOW
*St Nicholas with his
attendants rides
through the modern
streets of Amsterdam
on his way to the royal
palace.*

The procession, amid much cheering and ringing of church bells, is led by a police motorcade and a brass band. Then comes St Nicholas on horseback, wrapped in his scarlet cloak, with Black Peter at his side. He is followed by the mayor and other dignitaries of the city, decorated floats, a cavalcade of students and more brass bands. The procession stops in the main square of Amsterdam in front of the royal palace, and St Nicholas is welcomed by the Queen.

An old Dutch song describes his arrival:

*Look, there is a steamer from faraway lands
It brings us Saint Nicholas; he's waving his hands
His horse is a-prancing on deck up and down,
The banners are waving in village and town.*

*Black Peter is laughing and tells every one,
"The good kids get sweets, the bad ones get none!"
Oh, please, dear Saint Nicholas, if Pete and you would
Just visit our house, for we all have been good.*

On St Nicholas' Day in the Netherlands, the whole family waits in eager anticipation. Although the adults do not receive presents, it is a holiday. The Dutch children leave their clogs outside filled with hay and carrots or sugar for St Nicholas' horse. They spread a sheet on the ground and await the arrival of St Nicholas and Black Peter. Suddenly, there is a knock at the door and sweets and fruit are thrown onto the sheet. St Nicholas has arrived and is heralded in by Black Peter, both imposing figures. St Nicholas questions the children closely to

ABOVE
St Nicholas and Peter on a typical Dutch rooftop as they perform their seasonal duties. Peter, dressed *in his 16th-century clothing, looks rather unsteady and Santa stretches out a hand to help.*

make sure that they have been good. Black Peter carries a bag in which to take away the bad children, although in fact he never does so. St Nicholas goes away promising to return with the children's presents. After he has gone, the children go to bed after once again filling their shoes with hay and carrots. In the morning the carrots and hay have been replaced with gifts, and chairs have been overturned, showing that St Nicholas has been there. A naughty child might only receive a switch, and he or she just has to be thankful for not being carried off to Spain by Black Peter.

There is an old Dutch verse dedicated to St Nicholas as a gift-bringer that was often chanted by Dutch children:

Saint Nicholas, my dear good friend
To serve you ever was my end.
If you will, now, me something give,
I'll serve you ever while I live.

The Dutch were the first people to colonize successfully the Eastern seaboard of North America and settle in the New World. In the first Dutch colony of New Amsterdam on Manhattan Island, and later in the colonies along the shores of the Hudson River, they presumably celebrated their feasts in the traditional way.

The Christmas Number.

ST NICHOLAS

FOR·YOUNG·FOLKS

CONDUCTED BY

MARY·MAPES·DODGE

THE·CENTURY·CO·UNION·SQUARE·NEW·YORK
T·FISHER·UNWIN·PATERNOSTER·S^O·LONDON

COPYRIGHT, 1894, BY THE CENTURY CO. ENTERED AT THE POST-OFFICE AT NEW YORK AS SECOND-CLASS MAIL MATTER.

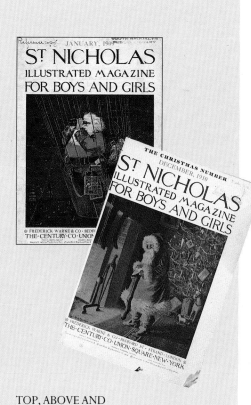

JANUARY, 1909

ST NICHOLAS

ILLUSTRATED MAGAZINE

FOR BOYS AND GIRLS

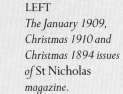

FREDERICK WARNE & CO · BEDF
THE·CENTURY·CO·UNION

THE CHRISTMAS NUMBER
DECEMBER, 1910

ST NICHOLAS

ILLUSTRATED MAGAZINE

FOR BOYS AND GIRLS

FREDERICK WARNE & CO · BEDFORD ST · STRAND · LONDON
THE·CENTURY·CO·UNION·SQUARE·NEW·YORK

TOP, ABOVE AND
LEFT
*The January 1909,
Christmas 1910 and
Christmas 1894 issues
of* St Nicholas
magazine.

CHAPTER THREE

ST NICHOLAS GOES WEST

On a bank high above the Hudson River in upstate New York is the house in which Washington Irving (1783–1859), the famous American writer, lived. Surrounded by lawns and densely wooded slopes, the house and land are swathed by the mist that rises up from the river. It can be a fanciful, mysterious place and it is here that Washington Irving wrote *The Legend of Sleepy Hollow* and his other stories which are so popular. What is not so well known is how instrumental he was in bringing us the image of Santa Claus that we are so familiar with today.

It is generally assumed that when the Dutch emigrated to America and established New Amsterdam, now New York City, they took their customs with them, especially the custom of celebrating St Nicholas' Day. A Charles W Jones, writing in the *New-York Historical Society Quarterly Bulletin* in October 1954, stated that there are very few actual references existing to the Dutch celebrations. Maybe this is true of the more public parades, but it is hard to believe that the Dutch children

were suddenly deprived of their visit from St Nicholas on 6 December. Mr Jones forcefully concluded his work with the words "Without Washington Irving there would be no Santa Claus". "Santa Claus", he continues, "was *made* by Washington Irving". And perhaps it is true that without Washington Irving we would not know about Santa.

There seems little doubt, however, that Dutch children awaited the coming of St Nicholas on 6 December in New Amsterdam as their parents had done in the Old. It is also a fact that other groups of settlers knew of him and associated him with gift-giving on the same day, on 25 December or at New Year's. A woodcut commissioned by the New-York Historical Society, and printed on a broadside in 1810, shows what he must have looked like in the Dutch days. He stands tall and proud in his bishop's robes, holding a purse in one hand and a birch in the other. He is accompanied by a beehive and a dog. Beside him are two children. One is a Good child, cherubic, with a stocking full of presents. The other is a Bad, sad child,

LEFT
An engraving, based on a painting by C R Leslie, of the famous American writer Washinton Irving, author of The Legend of Sleepy Hollow. *Irving was perhaps the most important person in bringing tales of Santa Claus to America.*

RIGHT
A familiar scene of Santa Claus filling the stockings hanging by the fireplace. But in this engraving, the artist has portrayed Santa as looking very much like one of the Dutch settlers in New York.

LEFT
St Nicholas riding through the air and dropping present down to the inhabitants of a new American town, the Dutch settlers' ships in the background.

spiteful, with a switch made of birch rods. Not featured in the illustration is Black Peter, who seems not to have made the transatlantic journey.

THE GUARDIAN OF NEW YORK

The picture most of us have of the Dutch in the New World and their St Nicholas celebrations actually comes from a book called *Knickerbocker's History of New York,* written in 1809 by Washington Irving. The book was supposedly written by a venerable Dutchman who went by the name of Diedrich Knickerbocker and was actually a satire. Apparently it had the New Yorkers roaring with laughter!

In *Knickerbocker's History,* the Dutch are pictured coming over on the boat the *Goede Vrouw* with the popular saint's image on the prow; and, of course, they name the first church after him. The saint is depicted as one of the Dutch themselves, with a broad-brimmed hat, short, wide breeches and smoking a long Dutch pipe!.

As Washington Irving says:

> *To this end they built a fair and goodly chapel within a fort, which they consecrated to his name; whereupon he immediately took the town of New Amsterdam under his peculiar patronage, and he has ever since been and I devoutly hope will ever be, the tutelar saint of this excellent city. At this early period was instituted that pious ceremony, still religiously observed in all our ancient families of the right breed, of hanging up a stocking in the chimney on St Nicholas eve; which stocking is always found in the morning miraculously filled – for the good St Nicholas has ever been a great giver of gifts . . .*

There are about two dozen references to St Nicholas in the Knickerbocker history. Perhaps the closest to our image of Santa Claus is the following description of him coming down the chimney:

> *. . . and as of yore, in the better days of man, the deities were wont to visit him on earth and bless his rural habitations, so, we are told, in the sylvan days of New Amsterdam, the good St Nicholas would often make his appearance in his beloved city, of a holiday afternoon, riding jollily among the tree-tops, or over the roofs of the houses, now and then drawing forth magnificent presents from his breeches-pockets, and dropping them down the chimneys of his favourites. Whereas, in these degenerate days of iron and brass, he never shows us the light of his countenance, nor ever visits us, save one night of the year, when he rattles down the chimneys of the descendants of patriarchs, confining his presents merely to the children, in token of the degeneracy of the parents.*

LEFT
An early Thomas Nast drawing of Santa Claus on Christmas eve waiting for the children to go to sleep before he delivers the presents. Notice the long Dutch clay pipe that Santa is smoking.

ABOVE
A rather later picture than the one on the left (and not by Nast), but Santa is still holding a long pipe and has an impish gleam in his eye.

Twenty-six years after he had written *Knickerbocker's History of New York,* Washington Irving was still very taken with St Nicholas and his image of Dutch colonial life. He helped form a literary society in New York in 1835, which met on 6 December to honour the famous saint. Washington Irving was its first secretary and he held meetings at his house in Sleepy Hollow. At that meeting and many others, long Dutch pipes were smoked and other early Dutch customs observed. Irving still described the saint as the guardian of New York.

Washington Irving created a new popularity for the bishop. With typical writer's vision he saw St Nicholas in America not in clerical robes but as a jolly fellow, like the good Dutch burghers. Instead of St Nicholas arriving on a white horse, he rode over the tree-tops, dropping presents down chimneys.

A best-selling author, Washington Irving's description of the saint rapidly became known to New Yorkers. The English settlers enthusiastically adopted the joyful Dutch celebrations of St Nicholas' Day, but they gradually merged them with their own emphasis on celebrating Christmas or the New Year. It is not hard to see how *Sinter Klaas* easily became Santa Claus in the mouths of the English-speaking New Yorkers.

Even today Washington Irving's house is open to the public, and at Christmas visitors can participate in a traditional American Christmas.

'TWAS THE NIGHT ...

There were many other stages in the transformation of the saintly bishop into our jolly benefactor, but the next step was one of the most crucial. In 1823 on 23 December, a poem entitled *An Account of a Visit from St Nicholas* was published, anonymously, in the Troy, New York, *Sentinel*. It was introduced by a preface written by the editor of the paper, Orville L Holley, who said:

We know not to whom we are indebted for the following description of that unwearied patron of music – that homely and delightful personage of parental kindness, Santa Claus, his costumes, and his equipage, as he goes about visiting the firesides of this happy land laden with Christmas bounties; but from whomsoever it may have come, we give thanks for it. There is, to our apprehension, a spirit of cordial goodness in it, a playfulness of fancy and benevol_____ ___y to enter into the feelings and promote ___ ___es of children which are altogether

_____ classic line, now usually rendered "'Twas ___ ___tmas", the poem was apparently written ___ C Moore for his six small children the ___ read it to them on 22 December. Some ___ copied it down and that a friend, who ___ it and submitted it for publication. ___ in 1779, and a professor of Biblical ___tion of Scripture in New York City, ___ be an unlikely author of such a piece.

ABOVE
The cover from an early edition of Clement C Moore's poem A Visit of St Nicholas.

LEFT
The Thomas Nast illustration of A Visit of St Nicholas *entitled "'Twas the night before Christmas, and all through the house/ Not a creature was stirring,* not even a mouse".

ABOVE
A particularly charming picture of Santa on the cover of another edition of A Visit of St Nicholas.

A Visit of St Nicholas

'Twas the night before Christmas when all through the house
Not a creature was stirring not even a mouse;
The stockings were hung by the chimney with care,
In hopes that St Nicholas soon would be there.
The children were nestled all snug in their beds,
While visions of sugarplums danced through their heads.
And Mama in her 'kerchief and I in my cap
Had just settled our brains for a long winter's nap,
When out on the lawn there arose such a clatter,
I sprang from my bed to see what was the matter.
Away to the window I fled like a flash,
Tore open the shutters and threw up the sash.
The moon on the breast of the new fallen snow
Gave the luster of midday to the objects below.

When what to my wandering eyes should appear
But a miniature sleigh and eight tiny reindeer.
With a little old driver so lively and quick
I knew in a moment it must be St Nick.
More rapid than eagles his coursers they came,
And he whistled and shouted and called them by name:
"Now, Dasher! now Dancer! now Prancer! and Vixen!
On Comet! on Cupid! on Donder and Blitzen!
To the top of the porch! to the top of the wall;
Now dash away! dash away! dash away all!"
As dry leaves that before the wild hurricane fly
When they meet with an obstacle mount to the sky,
So up to the housetop the coursers they flew,
With the sleigh full of toys and St Nicholas too.

And then in a twinkling I heard on the roof
The prancing and pawing of each little hoof—
As I drew in my head and was turning around,
Down the chimney St Nicholas came with a bound.
He was dressed all in furs from his head to his foot,
And his clothes were all tarnished with ashes and soot.
A bundle of toys he had on his back
And he looked like a peddler opening his pack;
His eyes – how they twinkled! His dimples how merry.
His cheeks were like roses, his nose like a cherry!
His droll little mouth was drawn up in a bow,
And the beard on his chin was as white as the snow;
The stump of a pipe he held tight in his teeth,
And the smoke it encircled his head like a wreath;

He had a broad face and a little round belly,
That shook when he laughed like a bowlful of jelly.
He was chubby and plump, a right jolly old elf,
And I laughed when I saw him in spite of myself;
A wink of his eye and a twist of his head
Soon gave me to know I had nothing to dread;
He spoke not a word but went straight to his work
And filled all the stockings, then turned with a jerk,
And laying his finger aside of his nose
And giving a nod up the chimney he rose.
He sprang to his sleigh, to his team gave a whistle,
And away they all flew like the down of a thistle;
But I heard him explain ere he drove out of sight:
"Merry Christmas to all, and to all a goodnight".

RIGHT
The opening page of the poem from a nicely illustrated edition of A Visit of St Nicholas.

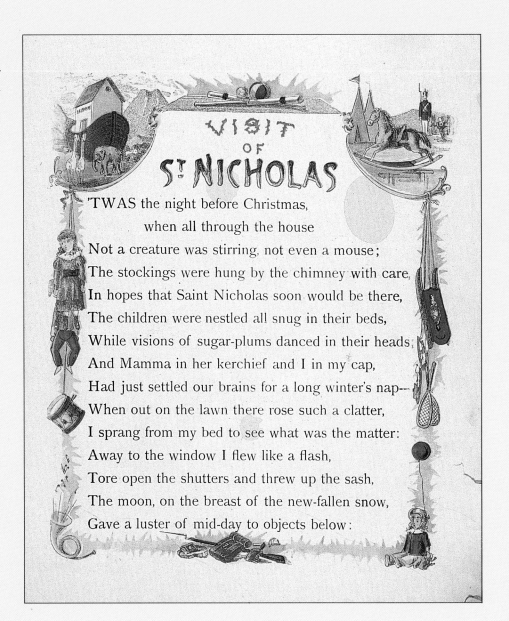

VISIT OF St NICHOLAS

'TWAS the night before Christmas,
when all through the house
Not a creature was stirring, not even a mouse;
The stockings were hung by the chimney with care,
In hopes that Saint Nicholas soon would be there,
The children were nestled all snug in their beds,
While visions of sugar-plums danced in their heads,
And Mamma in her kerchief and I in my cap,
Had just settled our brains for a long winter's nap---
When out on the lawn there rose such a clatter,
I sprang from my bed to see what was the matter:
Away to the window I flew like a flash,
Tore open the shutters and threw up the sash,
The moon, on the breast of the new-fallen snow,
Gave a luster of mid-day to objects below:

LEFT
A drawing by the famous illustrator Arthur Rackham for A Visit of St Nicholas, *entitled "And giving a nod, up the chimney he rose."*

TOP AND BOTTOM RIGHT
Pages from a modern edition of A Visit of St Nicholas.

Whether the originator or not, Clement C Moore had taken the story of the visit of St Nicholas as a basis, and told of a Santa Claus who would become one of the most famous of all folklore figures.

In the poem it is easy to see how Professor Moore adopted everyday items not only to enhance St Nicholas' image as a magical figure, but also to make him more believable. The clogs that the Dutch children left in the chimney corner on 6 December became instead something all children could relate to in cold weather – stockings.

THE SLEIGH AND REINDEER

RIGHT
*There can hardly be a
more delightful sight
than a horse-drawn
sleigh among snow-
covered trees.*

The sleigh and horse with its bells was a common means of transport in New England, where snow at Christmas was more likely than not. The joy of sleigh riding cannot be better described than by Mr Howard Paul, who was writing before Christmas 1855:

*There is generally snow on the ground at this time; if
Nature is amiable, there is sure to be; and a Christmas
sleigh-ride is one of those American delights that defy
rivalry. There is no withstanding the merry chimes of the
bells and a fleet passage over the snow-skirted roads. Towns
and countries look as if they had arisen in the morning in
robes of unsullied white. Every housetop is spangled with
the bright element: soft flakes are coquetting in the*

*atmosphere, and a pure mantle has been spread on all sides
that fairly invites one to disport upon its gleaming surface.*

*We abide quietly within our pleasant home on either the
eve or night of Christmas. How the sleighs glide by in rapid
glee, the music of the bells and the songs of the
excursionists falling on our ears in very wildness. We strive
in vain to content ourselves. We glance at the cheerful fire,
and hearken to the genial voices around us. We
philosophize and struggle against the tokens of merriment
without; but the restraint is torture. We, too, must join the
revellers, and have a sleigh-ride. Girls, get on your fur;
wrap yourselves up warmly in the old bear-skin; hunt up
the old guitar; the sleigh is at the door, the moon is beaming.
The bells tinkle and away we go!*

Old SANTECLAUS with much delight
His reindeer drives this frosty night,
O'er chimney tops, and tracks of snow,
To bring his yearly gifts to you.

Santa's sleigh flying was first described by Washington Irving. And for it to be pulled by reindeer gave St Nick an exotic link with the far north – a land of cold and snow where few, if any, people travelled and was hence mysterious and remote. The reindeer, however, were not first told of by Irving. In a publication called *The Children's Friend* a writer had described in 1821 "Old Sante Claus with much delight, His reindeer drives this frosty night". However, Clement C Moore told of eight reindeer and gave their names.

The immigrants to the New World must all have recognized something familiar in the little figure of St Nick. His fur costume would suggest *Pelz-Nicol* to a Bavarian, and the little gnome-like figure *Jule-nissen* to a Scandinavian. His elfish qualities rang bells with other nationalities too, for example the

ABOVE
*A Tuck relief print
unusually showing
Santa Claus in a sleigh
drawn by horses.*

RIGHT
*Santa sets out from his
Arctic home to deliver
presents around the
world, the Northern
Lights glowing behind
him.*

LEFT AND RIGHT
Santa has been drawn using many forms of transport, including modern vehicles such as cars and aircraft. These two drawings show what were the most modern forms of transport of their times.

Irish with their tradition of the "little people". In many ways, Santa was recognizable for many people, which probably helps to explain why he was adopted so readily – a new, but familiar, symbol for a new country.

One of the most interesting changes was in the physical transformation of St Nicholas. Even the original St Nicholas did not appear as the young, ascetic boy associated with the saint's stories, but as a white-bearded prelate. Now he had become a jolly, rotund Santa Claus of elf-like stature. Of course Washington Irving had already led the way in describing the saint's appearance, and Dr Moore was just building on this. One story says that Dr Clement Moore was also inspired by a short, chubby Dutch friend of his, who had sat by the fire telling stories of St Nicholas.

The other important thing that Moore's poem did was to tell of St Nick's arrival on Christmas Eve rather than St

A merry Christmas

Merry Christmas Greetings From Virginia

LEFT AND BOTH
FAR LEFT
*Pictures of Santa
usually show him as
merry and laughing,
but some show him
sad, stern or even
angry.*

LEFT
*A series of three Tuck
relief prints showing
Santa Claus figures
heavily laden with
toys.*

Nicholas' Eve. Of course, not everyone accepted this immediately; for many years some people still waited for the visit on 5 December or even New Year's Eve.

Although the images are so vivid, Moore's poem is not really very good as a poem and he was only too aware of this. He felt very strongly that it would hurt his reputation as a Professor of Divinity, and he did not acknowledge authorship of it until he included it in a collection of his poems published in 1844. Despite his personal feelings, it certainly captured the imagination of the public and was read in all parts of America. The poem succeeds because of its great conviction, spontaneous simplicity, perfect timing and the way in which everyday details are used.

Just as the poem did not immediately change the date on which everyone expected St Nick's arrival, so for a while in the nineteenth century, in engravings and drawings, the saint was still depicted in a variety of shapes and sizes. He appears severe as well as jovial, and still wears the bishop's cross, feathers in hat and fur coats. *A Visit of St Nicholas* did start a whole spate of poems, songs and stories about the gift-bringer, which all helped to solidify and broaden people's idea of Santa, such as the following one by a Mrs C S Stone.

Sly Santa Claus

All the house was asleep,
    And the fire burning low,
When, from far up the chimney,
    Came down a "Ho! ho!"
And a little, round man,
    With a terrible scratching,
Dropped into the room
    With a wink that was catching.
Yes, down he came, bumping,
And thumping, and jumping,
    And picking himself up without a sign of a bruise!

"Ho! ho!" he kept on,
    As if bursting with cheer,
"Good children, gay children,
    Glad children, see here!
I have brought you fine dolls,
    And gay trumpets, and rings,
Noah's arks, and bright skates,
    And a host of good things!
I have brought a whole sackful,
A packful, a hackful!
    Come hither, come hither, come hither and choose!

"Ho! ho! What is this?
    Why, they are all asleep!
But their stockings are up,
    And my presents will keep!
So, in with the candies,
    The books, and the toys;
All the goodies I have
    For the good girls and boys.
I'll ram them, and jam them,
And slam them, and cram them;
    All the stockings will hold while the tired youngsters snooze".

All the while his round shoulders
    Kept ducking and ducking;
And his little, fat fingers
    Kept tucking and tucking;
Until every stocking
    Bulged out, on the wall,
As if it were bursting,
    And ready to fall,
And then, all at once,
    With a whisk and a whistle,
And twisting himself
    Like a tough bit of gristle,
He bounced up again,
Like the down of a thistle,
    And nothing was left but the prints of his shoes.

There were still examples of the two names being used interchangeably, as in the following old song, which is anonymous.

Jolly Old Saint Nicholas

Jolly old Saint Nicholas
     Lean your ear this way!
Don't you tell a single soul
     What I am going to say;
Christmas Eve is coming soon;
     Now you dear old man,
Whisper what you'll bring to me;
     Tell me if you can.

When the clock is striking twelve,
     When I'm fast asleep,
Down the chimney broad and black,
     With your pack you'll creep;
All the stockings you will find
     Hanging in a row;
Mine will be the shortest one,
     You'll be sure to know.

Johnny wants a pair of skates;
     Susy wants a sled;
Nellie wants a picture book;
     Yellow, blue and red;
Now I think I'll leave to you
     What to give the rest;
Choose for me, dear Santa Claus
     You will know the best.

ABOVE
An 1899 cover of St Nicholas *magazine showing a somewhat stylized Santa Claus with two impish children dressed in an early Colonial style.*

RIGHT
The 1923 Christmas edition of St Nicholas *magazine shows Santa being caught in the act of delivering presents. The picture shows the kind of humour associated with Thomas Nast's drawings.*

A FAMILY FESTIVAL

Although most of the United States did not legally recognize Christmas until the latter half of the nineteenth century, by the 1840s it was already being seen very much as a children's festival, as these words from the editorial page of the magazine *Brother John* show.

Tomorrow will be Christmas, jolly, rosy Christmas, the Saturnalia of children. Ah, how the little rogues long for the advent of this day; for with it comes their generous friend Santa Claus with his sleigh, like the purse of Fortunatus, overflowing with treasures.

Part of the fuel for this new fervour for Christmas, or perhaps in response to it, was an American magazine for children called *St Nicholas,* which was published monthly from November 1873 to March 1940 (some covers from the magazine are shown on pages 30 and 31). Further issues appeared during 1943. It was extremely well regarded, and famous contributors included Louisa May Alcott, Frances Hodgson Burnett, Mark Twain, Robert Louis Stevenson and Rudyard Kipling.

The figure of Santa Claus rapidly became the focal point of Christmas as tales of him spread across America. Christmas was developing in the United States to become more and more of a family celebration, and as Santa Claus became less remembered for his religious origins he became more of a neutral focus for a polyglot society. Many different explanations have been put forward by historians and others for the large-scale adoption of Santa Claus.

RIGHT
The December 1900 edition of The Strand Magazine *shows Santa reading the very same edition of the magazine featuring himself. He seems to be enjoying the read!*

ALL THINGS TO ALL PEOPLES

Santa Claus struck a communal chord. As he was recognized as a general figure, rather than a religious one, Jews and those of other religions as well as Christians could adopt him and feel part of the same culture. The nineteenth century also saw the beginning of a materially richer society and Santa Claus was welcomed as a figure of unlimited bounty. Finally, he also became the symbol of what children expected from their parents, at a time when the importance of childhood as a stage in development was gaining greater recognition.

ABOVE

The centre pages from the 1890 December issue of The Christmas Puck, *showing Uncle Sam attending Christmas celebrations. Santa Claus is absent, and perhaps he would be out of place in this politically satirical drawing.*

It is interesting to look at a description of Christmas in America to see how a contemporary viewed Santa Claus at the end of the nineteenth century.

ABOVE
Santa Claus arrives on his sleigh to be greeted by a celebrating crowd in old fashioned dress. Published in 1900, this drawing is a reminder of the nostalgia associated with Santa Claus.

An old English legend was transplanted many years ago on the shores of America, that took root and flourished with wonderful luxuriance, considering it was not indigenous to the country. Probably it was taken over to New York by one of the primitive Knickerbockers, or it might have clung to some of the drowsy burgomasters who had forsaken the pictorial tiles of dear old Amsterdam about the time of Peter de Laar, or Il Bombaccia, as the Italians call him, got into disgrace in Rome. However this may be, certain it is that Santa Claus, or St Nicholas, the kind Patron-saint of the Juveniles, makes his annual appearance on Christmas Eve for the purpose of dispensing gifts to all good children. The festive elf is supposed to be a queer little creature that descends the chimney, viewlessly, in the deep hours of night, laden with gifts and presents, which he bestows with no sparing hand, reserving to himself a supernatural discrimination that he seems to exercise with every satisfaction. Before going to bed the children hang their newest stockings near the chimney, or pin them to the curtains of the bed. Midnight finds a world of hosiery waiting for favours; and the only wonder is that a single Santa Claus can get around among them all. The story goes that he never misses one, provided it belongs to a deserving youngster, and morning is sure to bring no reproach that the Christian Wizard has not nobly performed his wondrous duties.

FAR LEFT
LEFT AND ABOVE

Three of the famous advertisements created by Haddon Sundblom for Coca-Cola. Sundblom produced a long series of these popular images, which appeared from the 1930s onwards, and helped to solidify the image of Santa Claus we have today.

CHAPTER FOUR

THE VISUAL IMAGE OF SANTA CLAUS

*F*n 1837, a painting by Robert W Weir showed Santa as a friendly, tubby fellow, small but not elfin, wearing a hood and knee boots and carrying a bag of toys. He is grinning and in Moore's words "laying his finger aside of his nose". There were various other early pictures of Santa Claus. One by Sherwin and Smith shows him sitting by a fireplace putting toys in children's stockings. He is small, dressed in a fur coat and wearing a close-fitting cap with a bishop's cross on it. He is also smoking a small Dutch pipe. In another drawing, by J G Chapman in 1847, Santa Claus is a large figure, wearing fur-trimmed clothes with high boots and a feather in his cap.

THOMAS NAST AND SANTA

It was Thomas Nast, the famous American cartoonist, who crystallized for everyone the image we have of Santa Claus today.

Thomas Nast was born in 1840 in Landau, Bavaria, where his father was a musician. In 1846 his parents moved to America

SANTA CLAUS.

LEFT
A rare old book plate showing how Santa Claus was often depicted in the first part of the 19th century. He is a small, gnome-like figure, as always smoking his clay pipe.

LEFT
Thomas Nast, smiling and bearded, with a merry twinkle in eye. Nast was by far the most important illustrator in bringing us the image of Santa Claus we know and love so well today. Many of his drawings are shown in this book.

RIGHT
A cover for the
Harper's Weekly
Christmas
Supplement *of 1876*
by Thomas Nast.
Surrounded by images
from popular fairy
tales, the two children
seem neither amused
nor surprised by the
Santa Claus jack-in-
the-box.

RIGHT
Nast's first published
Santa Claus picture,
"A Visit from Saint
Nicholas". His early
images show Santa as
much more gnome-like
than the later ones.

and settled in New York. What was important for the future of Santa Claus was that they brought with them a great love of the elaborate German celebration of Christmas, which was to remain very dear to Thomas's heart. Thomas grew up to be a short, roly-poly person, and even by his late teens he could barely speak English. He did, however, know where his talents lay, and with great determination he trained as an artist at the National Academy of Design and became first a draughtsman at 15 and then an illustrator. During his highly successful career Nast was seen as a powerful political force, who used

his artistic skills to promote his strong feelings about contemporary issues. There was also a softer side to him, and from 1862 to 1886 he created a series of Christmas illustrations that were eagerly awaited by the public across America.

In 1862 Clement C Moore, the author of *A Visit of St Nicholas,* was finally persuaded at the age of 82 to acknowledge authorship of the popular poem and, in March of that year, to copy it down in his own handwriting. In the same year Thomas Nast was commissioned to do a series of drawings for *Harper's Illustrated Weekly* and his first illustration of Santa Claus appeared,

entitled *A Visit of St Nicholas.* In it Santa Claus is puffing on his pipe and his sleigh and reindeer are parked beside a snow-laden chimney pot, which he is about to go down. On his back he has a large bundle from which toys can be seen sticking out. In the background is a church spire and the moon, visible through the clouds, lights up the whole scene. From the composition of the picture it seems highly likely that Thomas Nast was familiar with Moore's poem. It was the first picture of Santa Claus as we know him today.

In the same issue in which Thomas Nast's first drawing of Santa Claus appeared, there was also a double-page spread on "Christmas Eve". This consisted of decorative drawings of a sentimental kind, which were very popular at the time. Wherever this issue of *Harper's Weekly* went it touched a responsive chord. It seemed that someone in every household had at some time experienced loneliness at Christmas. Thomas Nast's drawing of Santa – the figure of jollity and goodwill – represented what everyone wanted to experience at Christmas.

LEFT AND RIGHT
Two pictures of Santa by Thomas Nast, one showing the familiar scene of Santa about to descend a chimney, the other a more imaginative scene of Santa interviewing children in a cavern of ice, perhaps at the North Pole.

CHANGING PICTURES OF SANTA

Publishing was expanding; because of new technology printing was becoming less and less expensive and circulations of magazines were growing. There was great competition between the periodicals to produce the best pictures. Thomas Nast was the most talented of the contemporary illustrators, and he worked for Harper's for over 20 years. Although, today, we probably associate him with Christmas more than anything else, he also covered a wide range of subject matter. His illustrations were

ABOVE
A Nast picture entitled simply "Merry Christmas". Nast often used his own children as models for such drawings.

RIGHT
"Merry Old Santa Claus", a Thomas Nast wood engraving, shows Santa with an armful of toys, a crown of holly and holding his long pipe.

LEFT

The excitement and anticipation associated with Santa Claus leads one to expect a host of wonders and delights to be revealed when the curtain is drawn back in the Nast picture.

normally extremely satirical, but his Christmas work is his most heart-warming. Over the years the five Nast children were often used as models for the drawings, and many seasonal scenes from the Nast home were incorporated.

In 1890, Thomas Nast published a book called *Christmas Drawings for the Human Race,* which was a compilation of his work of the last 30 years, together with some new illustrations. Viewing the artist's work collectively (many of the pictures are reproduced in this book) it is interesting to see how his pictures

of Santa Claus changed considerably over the years. From the original fur-clad, gnome-like figure of the early drawings, to the full-size chap with a broad girth, flowing white locks, moustache and bewitching smile.

Nast was originally from Bavaria, and it is possible to see the elements of his homeland that he incorporated into the pictures. In one there is a fir tree behind Santa Claus and a landscape that resembles the Black Forest. As other props, he utilized many of the traditional trappings that we now auto-

ABOVE

Santa, with the aid of a telescope, spying on what the children are doing from a window in his house at the north pole. The idea for this illustration came from a drawing by Nast (see page 120).

RIGHT

Santa writing the names of the good children in an enormous book, with many more volumes on the shelves behind him. The idea for this picture came from a Nast drawing (see page 120).

ABOVE AND RIGHT
Nast's drawing of Santa using the new Edison telephone, entitled "'Hello, Santa Claus!' 'Hello, Little One!'" from Harper's Weekly.

matically associate with Christmas. Holly, mistletoe and other evergreens had been used since early Roman days for decorations in midwinter as symbols of everlasting life. To Christians, the holly wreath came to represent the passion of Christ, and mistletoe had always been renowned for its powers of healing.

Nast drew not only the gift-giving part of St Nick, but also his role as the rewarder of good children and the punisher of the naughty. Corporal punishment, however, was becoming less popular so no switch is in evidence in his pictures. Nast also was the first to point out that although Santa has always been old, he is also up to date. One of Nast's most charming pictures is of Santa using what was then the new invention of Edison's telephone. Children now had the novel option of calling up Santa instead of writing to him.

The North Pole as the location for Santa's home was also first drawn by Nast. Maybe it was suggested to him by Moore's reindeer and sleigh, and it does have certain advantages for Santa. It is such a remote place that no children can spy upon Santa at his work, but although inaccessible it is conveniently situated for travelling to all parts of the world. Another benefit of the North Pole as a home for Santa Claus is that no country could claim him as their own – he belongs to everyone.

The toys in Nast's pictures were, of course, those that were popular with children of the day. Endearing details, such as the spy glass that Santa uses to check up on the behaviour of boys and girls and the enormous record book that he keeps in which he listed all the good and bad children, provided character and substance to the drawings.

RIGHT

One of the common images of Santa Claus is of him in his workshop making toys. In this picture Santa seems happily absorbed, smoking his pipe and with a warm stove to keep out the arctic cold. Unusually, however, he is wearing a mixture of colours: both blue and red.

THE COLOUR OF CHRISTMAS

It is in depicting the figure of Santa Claus himself that Nast was most influential. He had portrayed Santa in various classic situations: in his toy workshop; driving his sleigh; going down a chimney; placing toys in stockings etc. All was going well, but Nast's artistic sense was not satisfied by drawing only Santa's brown, fur costume. Some of the illustrations were in colour, so Nast decided to show Santa in his brightest, most cheerful costume for a cold winter's night, and like the berries on the holly his outfit is brilliant red.

What made Nast stand out from his contemporary illustrators was not only the "vision" of Santa Claus that he had, but also the superb way that he conveyed the intense excitement and anticipation associated with Christmas and the visit of Santa Claus. Thomas Nast's work was also distinguished by his sense of humour. He used all the traditional themes associated with Christmas, but he added wit and made a picture a story. For example, in *A Chance to Test Santa's Generosity* (see page 19), which was published in 1876, a child is seen hanging up an enormous stocking. One of his best pictures is one in which Santa does not actually appear but is about to, and is entitled *Not a creature was stirring not even a mouse* (see page 43), a line from Clement C Moore's poem. Every detail of the mice's life is complete in miniature, from the tiny beds to the Christmas bric-a-brac in their room within a room.

RIGHT
*Santa taking a glass of
champagne with a
cherub. An unlikely
scene perhaps, but
surely even Santa
needs to relax with a
suitable celebration
after another
successful Christmas
season of hard work.*

LEFT AND RIGHT
The spirit of goodwill and generosity associated with Santa Claus is of great appeal to advertisers as something to associate with commercial products. Two examples are given here, and see also the pictures on pages 60 and 61.

CHRISTMAS CARDS

Between the 1840s and the 1870s great strides were made in the mechanical reproduction of pictures in colour, which enabled Christmas cards – first made in 1843 – to be printed in large numbers, and therefore profitably. Once they appeared at a reasonable price more people could afford them and indulge in the new way of exchanging greetings. The cards varied tremendously in style and design, but they also helped to fix the image of Santa for people and to suggest his flexibility and adaptability. Pictures of Santa began to be seen not just as a symbol of Christmas, but also as a powerful way to convey a message. At the turn of the century, some Christmas cards seemed to have forgotten the purpose of the season altogether and were very often little more than advertisements.

THIS PAGE AND
NEXT
*Seven old Christmas
cards, all featuring
Santa Claus, a
favourite theme. His
costume varies
considerably — in
colour and in other*
*ways — and Santa
himself varies between
being a kindly
patriarch and the
more jolly figure we
know today.*

Merry Christmas

A Merry Christmas

A MERRY CHRISTMAS

CHAPTER FIVE

THE NEWS OF SANTA CLAUS SPREADS

In England the name "Santa Claus" is now synonymous with "Father Christmas", which is what he was known as long before the arrival of the American name.

MUMMERS' PLAYS

Father Christmas was depicted in the mummers' plays, which were performed, in various versions, in villages at Christmas time, but this custom had virtually died out by the nineteenth century. Images of him, however, go back even farther than that. He appeared in the Tudor and Stuart court masques, and in the fifteenth century there was a carol that begins "Hail Father Christmas, hail to thee". In Ben Jonson's *The Masque of Christmas* he appears with the following members of his family: Missrule, Caroll, Minced-Pie, Gambol, Post-and-Pair, New Year's Gift, Mumming, Wassall, Offering and Baby Cake.

In the mid-seventeenth century, a writer described him as an "old, old very old greybearded gentleman called Christmas, who was wont to be a very familiar guest and visit all sorts of people both poor and rich". The mummers were descendants of the masquers. They were dressed rather like morris dancers still are today, with white trousers and waistcoats decorated with ribbons and handkerchiefs, and each carrying a drawn sword or cudgel. On their heads they had high caps of pasteboard, covered with fancy paper and adorned with beads, small pieces of looking-glass, bugles and streamers of coloured cloth. The character of Father Christmas was usually personified as a grotesque old man, wearing a great mask and wig, with a large club in his hand. He was also often portrayed wearing a crown of holly leaves.

A traditional mummers' play started with the words

In comes I, old Father Christmas
Welcome in or welcome not,
Sometimes cold and sometimes hot,
I hope Father Christmas will never be forgot.

ABOVE
*A group of 18th-
century mummers in
England perform in
front of a house near a*
*village in winter. The
occupants of the house
are gathered outside to
watch.*

ABOVE

*A group of masquers
arrive at the royal
court to perform, the
figure of Father*

*Christmas leading the
way with a large
"wassail" bowl.*

LEFT
A more homely scene as a band of mummers enters a house. The figure of Father Christmas, his head crowned with holly and a large branch of holly in his hand, stands to the front and announces their arrival.

Father Christmas was not given a very large role in these plays, and none of the responsibilities of Santa Claus. He just represented a general spirit of revelry and festivity. The name, however, was obviously a local alternative for the new creation from America, and in the tradition of true folklore the best from the past was combined with the new of the present.

By the first half of the nineteenth century the old Christmas customs had languished in England. Even the famous poet Alfred Lord Tennyson lamented the lost glory of the old-time Christmas. In 1842 he wrote:

The host and I sat round the wassail bowl
The halfway ebbed and there we held a talk —
How all the old honour had from Christmas gone
Or dwindled down to some old games
In some odd nooks like this.

Washington Irving visited England in 1820 and met Sir Walter Scott, who had read *Knickerbocker's History* and enjoyed it very much. It was during this visit that Washington Irving wrote his *Sketch Book*, which contains the remarkable description of a traditional Christmas at Bracegirdle Hall, Yorkshire, under the title *Old Christmas in Merrie England*. When Washington Irving's publisher went bankrupt, Sir Walter Scott introduced him to

"MERRY CHRISTMAS!"—DRAWN BY KENNY MEADOWS.

LEFT
A merry Victorian Christmas in England, the festivities in full swing.

ABOVE
Father Christmas, above scenes of celebration, gives greetings to all.

his own publisher, John Murray. Murray published the *Sketch Book* and it was a tremendous success. Washington Irving had immortalized a traditional Christmas not just for the Americans but for the English too.

THE ADOPTION OF SANTA

As in many other European countries, if presents were exchanged at this season it was usually done at New Year's Eve and they were between adults rather than for children. In the 1840s, however, there was an increasing emphasis on Christmas Day. This seems to have happened for several reasons. The press – which now reached a far wider audience with its cheaper production costs and consequently wider circulation – stressed the fact that Christmas Day was the celebration of the birth of Jesus. Birthdays had always been a day for giving presents and it was a natural step to celebrate Jesus' birth by giving gifts on that day.

Before Christmas had been banned by Oliver Cromwell from 1644 to 1660, there had been an old custom of giving sweets and small presents to children on Christmas Day itself. This had virtually died out, but now the custom was enjoying a revival, in part because of the many articles that were being written in the Christmas editions of magazines about the "old traditions" of Christmas. Another influential element was that, just as in America, children were becoming a greater focus in society, and it seemed appropriate to use this time to give them greater emphasis.

The importation of the Christmas tree from Germany, and the accompanying rituals of gift-giving on Christmas Eve, gave

RIGHT
A late-19th-century English picture shows Santa Claus distributing gifts to children. He looks a more mysterious figure than that presented in American pictures at the time.

further impetus to the idea of presents. Santa Claus provided the final influence. By the end of the century Christmas Day was firmly fixed – in England at least – as a children's festival and the day on which presents were given.

Santa Claus or "Father Christmas" came back into English Christmas festivities when people were reminded of him from America, although few were aware of this. This injected new life into the English Christmas and was the answer to those who prayed that Father Christmas and his customs might be restored "to some portion of their ancient honours".

Welcome Father Christmas was the title of a penny booklet of recitations, enigmas, charades and puzzles produced in 1864. In the 1870s and 1880s references began to appear to a mysterious person who visited at Christmas time – on Christmas Eve to be precise – who was known variously as Santa Claus or Father Christmas. He was first adopted by the middle classes who saw him as a natural personification of their new fervour for a family celebration. His increasing significance can be seen by his appearance on Christmas cards in a variety of costumes and in such magazines as *Punch*.

LEFT

Santa arrives carrying an umbrella. Perhaps he is prepared for the notorious English weather!

BELOW

A message of heartfelt goodwill from a Santa who looks almost exhausted by his Christmas efforts.

CHIMNEYS AND STOCKINGS

The custom of stockings, chimneys and Christmas Eve visits was still very new in England in the 1880s. "I have not seen the following observance recorded anywhere", wrote Edwin Lees, a member of the Folklore Society, in *Note and Queries* in 1879,

> . . . On Christmas Eve, when the inmates of a house in the country retire to bed, all those desirous of a present place a stocking outside the door of their bedroom, with the expectation that . . . Santiclaus *will fill the stocking or place something within it before morning . . . . From what region of the earth or air this benevolent* Santiclaus *takes flight, I have not been able to ascertain but probably he may be heard of in other counties than those I have mentioned. An Exeter resident tells me this custom prevails also in Devonshire.*

ABOVE LEFT
A 19th-century picture shows Santa Claus stepping confidently into a chimney.

ABOVE
Although clearly a more modern picture than the one to the left, Santa's activities do not change.

RIGHT
The custom of hanging stockings by the fireplace spread to the United Kingdom from America and was widely adopted.

LEFT
Santa stands in a wintry landscape, a rabbit looking on.

RIGHT
The members of the Pickwick club in Charles Dickens' novel The Pickwick Papers *held almost ideal traditional Christmas celebrations.*

Although the poem *A Visit of St Nicholas* was not published in England until 1891, the spread of customs surrounding Santa Claus was swift. He is mentioned in a tableau by Josiah Booth, *A Christmas Party,* in 1884. In it Santa Claus was driven off by reindeer and in a baritone sang "Ten thousand homes", which tells how he will fill all the children's stockings:

> *Ten thousand homes are waiting*
> *The visits I shall pay;*
> *A hundred thousand children*
> *Are longing for the day.*
> *And early in the morning*
> *The stockings will be seized . . .*
> *The dolls and toys and trumpets,*
> *The gingerbread and cake,*
> *Will gladden all the young ones*
> *As festivals they make*

The name Father Christmas continued to appear. A part song called *Old Father Christmas,* published in 1894 as one of Novello's School Songs, illustrates:

> *Old Father Christmas is passing by,*
> *His cheeks are ruddy, he's bright of eye,*
> *His beard is white with the snow of time.*

American Santa Claus customs were described in detail in Susan Warner's best-selling story *The Christmas Stocking,* which was first published in London in the 1850s and went into several editions. It took a while for Santa to percolate fully into English life, but in the grim industrial society of Victorian England people were eager to look back to what they thought was a more perfect age, and to escape into a world of romance and sentimentality. Santa Claus also gave some people a wonderful opportunity for their philanthropic spirit.

Washington Irving had started the nostalgia for a traditional, charitable Christmas, but other writers were to feed it even more. Charles Dickens also produced a literary picture of the ideal traditional Christmas, with his description in *The Pickwick Papers* of the season at Dingley Dell. Even more influential were the series of Christmas books that he brought out – there can hardly be a single person who has not heard of *A Christmas Carol* with its main character Scrooge. Sympathy for the under-privileged at the end of the nineteenth century was to prove a best-selling line in literature, art and religion.

CHRISTMAS CHARITY

Santa Claus is, of course, the ultimate gift-giver. He became a figure for concentrating the charitable ambitions of those who were concerned about the great divide in society between the "haves and the have nots", which was more obvious at Christmas than at any other time of the year.

Christian ladies in London in the 1890s dressed up as Santa

Claus to distribute some Christmas cheer to the poor. The Santa Claus Distribution Fund was inaugurated in 1894 to provide presents and clothing for poor children. Their official organ, *The Santa Claus Gazette,* cost a penny. Endorsed by royalty, it exhorted its subscribers to contribute to the fund. It pledged to provide each poor child with "a separate Parcel and each Parcel is labelled and ADDRESSED TO THE CHILD and delivered at the home on Christmas Eve . . .. EACH PARCEL CONTAINS – One Garment or useful article of clothing; one Toy or Doll; a Bag or Box of Sweets; and a Christmas Card". Despite the efforts of the Fund – by 1910 they were distributing 10,000 parcels at Christmas – there were never enough of these charitable "Santa Clauses" to reach all the poor.

Santa Claus was the same magical figure for the children in England as he was in America. The custom of hanging up a stocking became just as popular, although in England stockings are more commonly hung at the end of the bed. Some children have even become so greedy that they have substituted a pillowcase for the stocking. Not only was it customary to hang up a stocking, but tradition also determined what Santa put in it. At one time there was always a plump, rosy apple in the toe for health and happiness, and an orange in the heel – until this century oranges were a luxury item. The rest was filled with small items such as whistles, sheets of picture scraps, packets of coloured beads, balls of Berlin wool for making reins or working texts, apples, sweets and pink sugar mice. Today stockings are usually filled with small gifts, but also often with much more expensive items.

RIGHT
*Santa Claus gives a
doll to a child who has
fallen asleep while
waiting for his arrival.*

BELOW
*This time the children
are wide awake and
waiting as Santa comes
through the door.*

97

LEFT
Kriss Kringle, simply
another name for
Santa, unpacking toys
ready to load into the
stockings hanging by
the fireplace.

CHAPTER SIX

SANTA CLAUS
THE
GIFT-GIVER

Celebrations around the midwinter solstice had been used for gift-giving since Roman times. At their winter festival – called the Saturnalia because they worshipped Saturn as the god of everything that grew – the Romans had a public holiday that lasted for a week. Everyone took part in the feasting and games. Even the slaves were made free for a day and allowed to say and do what they liked. People exchanged presents, a custom called *Strenae,* as a symbol of goodwill. At first these were green boughs from the grove of the goddess Strenia. Later gifts were given of sweet pastries to ensure a pleasant year, precious stones, coins of gold or silver to symbolize wealth and, the most popular of all, candles as a symbol of warmth and, light. As the Roman Empire spread so did this custom of gift-giving to other parts of the world. Because the Saturnalia marked the beginning of a new year, in most countries presents were given on New Year's Day, not Christmas Day. The advent and spread of Christianity generally caused the gift-giving to be moved to other times of the year.

LEFT
A child stretches eagerly for a toy offered by Santa Claus, who is dressed more in the manner of St Nicholas than the familiar Santa.

A Merry Christmas

*A laughing Santa
Claus offers a
magnificent pile of gifts,
happy to be
performing what is his
main function.*

In Germany the packages of Christmas gifts were called "Christ-bundles" and often came in bundles of three. There was something rewarding, something useful and something for discipline. In the seventeenth century a typical bundle would contain candy, sugar plums, cakes, apples, nuts, dolls and toys. The useful things would be clothes, caps, mittens, stockings, shoes and slippers. The gifts "that belong to teaching, obedience and discipline" were items such as ABC tables, paper, pencils, books and the "Christ-rod". This rod, attached to the bundle, was a pointed reminder for good behaviour. Another way of presenting gifts was the old German custom of the "Christmas ship", in which bundles for children were stored away. To some extent this custom was also adopted in England, but never with the same degree of popularity.

BOXING DAY

English monarchs demanded Christmas gifts from their subjects. This was one of the ways in which Queen Elizabeth I replen-

RIGHT
A Santa-like figure rides on a pony with, in front of him, Christkindel *carrying a "tree of light" (see page 107).*

LEFT
A crib scene in Burkina Faso, made very much in the local style. All around the world familiar Christmas customs appear, even if in slightly altered form.

ished her wardrobe. Nobles, clergyman and all the palace servants each gave according to their means. Another popular Christmas custom in England was "boxing" on the feast of St Stephen, 26 December. It originated in medieval times when the priests would empty the alms boxes in all the churches on the day after Christmas, and distribute the gifts to the poor of the parish. In imitation of this church practice, the workers, apprentices and servants kept their own, personal "boxes" made of earthenware, in which they stored savings and donations throughout the year. At Christmas came the last and greatest flow of coins, collected from patrons, customers and friends. Then, on the day after Christmas, the box was broken and the money counted. This custom was eventually called "boxing" and came to mean the giving and accepting of presents at this time of year. Each present is a "box" and the day of present-giving is "boxing day". Although the concept of the master or the boss giving his workers a "box" has now died out, it still exists in an altered form. Both in the United States and in England, for example, many workers are still given a Christmas bonus in their pay.

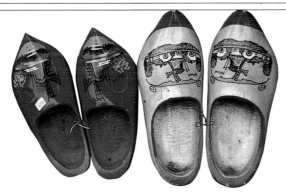

ABOVE
Traditional wooden shoes, in which Santa leaves his gifts in some countries.

RIGHT
The Festival of the Three Kings on 6th January in Spain. Children receive gifts from the Three Kings then, as well as from El Niño Jesus *on Holy Night.*

LEFT AND BELOW
Russian dolls in the form of Santas and three modern Santa figures in a variety of costumes. Santa Claus often appears in slightly different guises around the world.

A similar custom prevailed in Holland and some parts of Germany, where children were taught to save their pennies in a pig-shaped earthenware box. This box was not to be opened until Christmas and consequently was called the "feast-pig". From this custom we now have piggy-banks.

THE GIFT-GIVER AROUND THE WORLD

In the centuries before Santa Claus was well known, and still today in the many countries where he has not been widely adopted, the child Jesus is the gift-bringer. He comes with the angels during the night, trimming the tree and putting the presents under it.

In Spain and Spanish-speaking countries the child Jesus (*el Niño Jesus*) brings Christmas gifts for the children during Holy Night. He is found in the morning in the previously empty crib, and all the presents are arranged in front of it.

The German name of the Christ Child is *Christkind,* commonly used in its diminutive form *Christkindel*. The gifts of the

RIGHT
In both Russia and Italy, gifts are brought by a legendary old woman: a woman called Babushka *in Russia and one named* La Befana *in Italy.*

A MERRY CHRISTMAS

Christ Child are brought by his messenger, a young girl with a golden crown who holds a tiny "Tree of Light". Still today in America, "Kriss Kringle" – deriving from the German *Christkindel* – is another name used for Santa Claus.

Santa may appear under different names and in different guises. For example, French children leave their shoes by the fireplace on Christmas Eve so that they can be filled with gifts by *Père Noel*. In the morning they find that the shoes have been filled and that sweets, fruit, nuts and small toys have also been hung on the branches of the tree.

In Sweden the children wait eagerly for *Jultomten,* whose sleigh is drawn by the *Julbocker,* the goats of the thunder god Thor. With his red suit and cap, and a bulging sack on his back, he looks much like Santa Claus as we know him. In Denmark, too, the gift-bringer *Julemanden* carries a sack and is drawn by reindeer. Elves known as *Juul Nisse* come from the attic, where they live, to help with the chores during Yuletide. The children put a saucer of milk or rice pudding for them in the attic and are delighted to find it empty in the morning.

Gifts arrive in other ways too. The children in Poland receive their gifts from the stars, while in Hungary the angels

bring them. Children of Syria receive theirs from the Youngest Camel on 6 January, which is Three Kings' Day. The children of Spain, Mexico, Puerto Rico, the Philippines and South American countries also receive gifts at this time as well as on Holy Night, but from the Three Kings.

In Italy an unusual figure is the gift-bringer for children. It is the "Lady Befana" or "Bufana" (*La Befana*), the ageless wanderer. Apparently *La Befana* refused to go to Bethlehem with the wise men when they passed her door, and she has been searching for the Christ Child ever since. On the Eve of Three Kings' Day (Epiphany) she wanders from house to house, peering into the faces of the children and leaving gifts. On that day the children roam the streets, blowing their paper trumpets and receiving the gifts which *La Befana* has provided for them. Her name comes from the word "Epiphany".

The gift-bringer in Russia is also a legendary woman, called *Babushka* (Grandmother). She is said to have misdirected the

ABOVE
A relief print shows Santa as he discusses what the children want from his sleigh.

LEFT
Offering a gift, Santa strides busily on his way.

ABOVE
A relief print again shows Santa Claus giving children gifts from his sleigh.

RIGHT
Santa pulls presents from his sack to fill the stockings hung on the mantelpiece.

Magi when they inquired their way to Bethlehem. According to another version she refused hospitality to the Holy Family on its way to Egypt. Whatever her fault, she repented of her unkindness and to make reparation for her sin she now goes about the world on Christmas Eve, looking for the Christ Child and distributing gifts to the children. Another Russian legendary figure is *Kolya* (Nicholas – St Nicholas), who travels about during Holy Night, putting on window-sills little wheat cakes that have to be eaten on Christmas Day.

Easter is the main holiday in Greece and, although Christmas carols are sung and there are special Christmas foods, there are no Christmas trees and no presents. Presents are exchanged on St Basil's Day, who was one of the four founders of the Greek Orthodox Church.

All around the world, however, Santa Claus is becoming better and better known. He has become an international figure standing for charity, generosity and benevolence.

RIGHT

Santa checks in an enormous book listing children who have been good. Perhaps he is deciding which of the children should receive which toys.

SANTA TAKEN FOR GRANTED

Santa Claus is usually a totally benevolent figure, although in some guises he is more judgmental. Children are not going to have things all their own way with Santa.

Santa's New Idea

Said Santa Claus
One winter's night,
"I really think it's only right
That gifts should have a little say
'Bout where they'll be on Christmas Day".

So then and there
he called the toys
Intended for good girls and boys,
And when they'd settled down to hear,
He made his plan for them quite clear.

These were his words:
"Soon now", said he,
"You'll all be speeding off with me
To bring the Christmas joy and cheer
To little ones both far and near.

"Here's my idea,
It seems but fair
That you should each one have a share
In choosing homes where you will stay
On and after Christmas Day.

"Now the next weeks
Before we go
Over the miles of glistening snow
Find out the tots that you like best
And think much nicer than the rest".

The toys called out
"Hurrah! Hurrah!
What fun to live always and play
With folks we choose – they'll surely be
Selected very carefully".

So, children dear,
When you do see
Your toys in socks or on a tree,
You'll know in all the world 'twas you
They wanted to be given to.

From *The New Outlook* (Toronto),
December 1932.

ABOVE
Santa prepares the metal parts for toys he will make in his workshop.

RIGHT
The finishing touches. Santa carefully paints a dolls' house using a large palette of colours.

RIGHT
Santa, his bag of presents at the ready, asks, "What would you like for Christmas?"

BELOW
Even a snowstorm will not stop Santa Claus getting through with the presents for the children.

RIGHT
Another picture of Santa spying on what the good children are doing (compare with those on pages 72 and 120).

Another poem from the latter part of the last century, called *The Revolt of Santa Claus*, dealt with the problem that Santa Claus was being taken for granted, and had become so ubiquitous that he thought he should not make his annual visit any more. Then, one by one, children from nations around the world assured him of their love, and predicted universal disappointment if he did not make the trip. He was moved by the children's pleas and decided to visit mankind again.

The fact that Santa Claus was disenchanted with the world let people see a human quality in him. He was not so much an elf but more like a human being. Music and stories grew up about his annual visit. Song-books of 1890, 1899, 1908 and 1916 had such titles as *Santa Claus is Come to Town, Santa Claus*

RIGHT
Christmas Eve, and Santa, sack of presents at the ready and reindeer waiting outside, puts on his warm, fur-lined coat, ready for his big night of the year.

ABOVE
*Santa checks on his list
of children. Who has
he visited already and
who should he deliver
presents to next?*

Last Christmas Eve and *Old Santa Claus Sat All Alone*, and he also featured in many short stories.

Even as early as 1864 children seemed to be getting too selfish and acquisitive at Christmas. *Harper's Illustrated Weekly* published a report from "Santa Claus's Wish Council":

> *"Something must be done", said he, "different from what has ever been done before. The days when the reindeer and I could manage this kind of thing are over. One of Grant's wagon-trains could not carry the things I am expected to deliver. The days when a tiny stocking full of candy and nuts, a cake and a primer, or a squawking dog and a jumping-jack would satisfy a child, appear to have passed away for ever. Here's Fenella McFlimsey wants a gold tea set for her doll, and Katarina von Trondelbedde wants a velvet cloak and royal ermines. Does she indeed! I've a great mind to bring her a switch as I've done in old times! And forty thousand others as reasonable as they. Fact is, I won't stand it!" and the old fellow grew so warm that he threw off his mink dressing-gown, and kicked his slippers vigorously into one corner. "Blazius! Fetch me my buffalo skin capote, and see that the reindeer are ready in six seconds"; and the old gentleman flew round in a style quite astonishing for one of his age. "I'll see the parents themselves, and try to talk a little common sense into them".*

Some people have complained that the arrival of Santa Claus has robbed Christmas of its true meaning, but in fact it is the exact opposite. In the United States and England, and other countries that have adopted Santa, the nativity is seen as something apart from him. The secular and the religious aspects are separate, but the goodwill is shared by all.

THIS PAGE AND
NEXT
*More modern images
of Santa Claus, from
the 1950s onwards,
reflect modern trends
in graphic art,
although traditional
styles of image are still
commonly used.*

THIS PAGE AND PREVIOUS
While images may be modern, the themes remain the same and, of course, Santa stays the same jolly figure.

WISHING YOU A MERRY CHRISTMAS

CHAPTER SEVEN

DO YOU BELIEVE IN SANTA?

ABOVE
*A whole range of
Santa's activities all in
one drawing by
Thomas Nast.*

RIGHT
*Santa in his workshop,
a picture influenced by
the work of Nast.*

The classic response to whether Santa Claus exists or not was written by Francis Church, an editorial writer for the New York *Sun* in response to a letter from eight-year-old Virginia O'Hanlon.

Is There a Santa Claus?

By Francis P Church

We take pleasure in answering at once and thus prominently the communication below, expressing at the same time our great gratification that its faithful author is numbered among the friends of The Sun:

Dear Editor,

I am 8 years old.
Some of my little friends say there is no Santa Claus. Papa says "If you see it in The Sun it's so".
Please tell me the truth, is there a Santa Claus?

Virginia O'Hanlon
115 West 95th Street
New York City

Virginia, your little friends are wrong. They have been affected by the skepticism of a skeptical age. They do not believe except what they see. They think that nothing can be which is not comprehensible by their little minds. All minds, Virginia, whether they be men's or children's, are little. In this great universe of ours man is a mere insect, an ant, in his intellect, as compared with the boundless world about him, as measured by the intelligence capable of grasping the whole of truth and knowledge.

Yes, Virginia, there is a Santa Claus. He exists as certainly as love and generosity and devotion exist, and you know that they abound and give to your life its highest beauty and joy. Alas! how dreary would be the world if there was no Santa Claus! It would be as dreary as if there were no Virginias. There would be no childlike faith, then, no poetry, no romance to make tolerable this existence. We should have no enjoyment, except in sense and sight. The eternal light with which childhood fills the world would be extinguished.

Not believe in Santa Claus! You might as well not believe in fairies! You might get your papa to hire men to watch in all the chimneys on Christmas Eve to catch Santa Claus, but even if they did not see Santa Claus coming down what would that prove? Nobody sees Santa Claus but that is no sign that there is no Santa Claus. The most real things in the world are those that neither children nor men can see. Did you ever see fairies dancing on the lawn? Of course not, but that's no proof that they are not there. Nobody can conceive or imagine all the wonders there are unseen and unseeable in the world.

You tear apart the baby's rattle and see what makes the noise inside, but there is a veil covering the unseen world which not the strongest man, nor even the united strength of all the strongest men that ever lived, could tear apart. Only faith, fancy, poetry, love, romance can push aside that curtain and view and picture the supernal beauty and glory beyond. Is it real? Ah, Virginia, in all this world there is nothing else real and abiding.

No Santa Claus! Thank God he lives, and lives forever. A thousand years from now, Virginia, nay, ten times ten thousand years from now, he will continue to make glad the heart of childhood.

MANY SANTAS?

With the proliferation of Santas in stores and on street corners it is often difficult to explain to inquisitive, observant children how there happen to be so many of him. The answer is that because Santa is so terribly busy he allows other kind people to help him out.

Many are the stories of Santa's activities. One of the more famous is of the Magic Dust. This explains how brightly wrapped packages can appear under the Christmas tree before Santa has made his visit on Christmas Eve and many other wonderful things. Santa's pockets are filled with an unlimited amount of magic dust, which he uses to make possible all the seemingly impossible things that he does each Christmas Eve. For example, his reindeer can fly. One man can visit every good child's home around the world on a single night. Just a few large brown sacks can carry every toy that every child has asked for.

It is an easy task for the magic dust to fill the empty packages that parents, aunts, uncles and grandparents have placed under the tree with just the right presents. This same dust explains why no child has ever seen Santa Claus. Try as they might to stay awake on Christmas night a few specks of the magic dust makes them doze right off.

LETTERS TO SANTA

One of the most important things to do before Christmas is to write to Santa Claus telling him what you want. Some books now advise children on how to write the most persuasive letter! You should let Santa himself decide whether you have

been good and deserve a visit. They say you should promise food and warm drink when he arrives, but most important of all, you should tell him what you would like for Christmas.

There are different things to do with the letters once they have been written. In Germany, where the children write to the *Christkind,* they leave their letters, decorated with glue and

RIGHT
Santa looks at a map of the world, wondering how he is going to manage his visits to all of the children this year.

ABOVE

Something to eat and drink and a message of good wishes left ready for Santa's visit.

RIGHT

Santa stands in his wonderful storeroom of presents making a list of which gifts will go to each child.

sprinkled with sugar to make them sparkle, on the window-sill. In most countries they used to throw them on the fire so that they would go up the chimney – the same one that Santa comes down. The letters should burn and the charred remains should float gently up. In *What Katy Did* they are having a spot of trouble getting the letters to "fly up". Katy unobtrusively opens the door, creating a draft, and the letters go shooting up the chimney.

With the advent of central heating, open fires are far less common than they once were and children have to use other measures. Some make use of the postal or mail service and pop their letters into the official boxes. Enterprising stationers have even produced a special set of writing paper and envelopes designed specifically for letters to Santa.

Children often ask questions about Santa's life and where he lives. Most people agree he lives in a wooden house high in the trees in the far north. There he is helped by his elves, who create all manner of toys and other gifts in his workshops. The reindeer live in stables, and in the weeks before Christmas they are given extra large helpings of moss and hay, which build them up so that they are strong enough to pull the sleigh. After Christmas Eve, when the reindeer are utterly exhausted, they are allowed to have a long rest to recuperate.

The food that it is advised to leave for Santa varies from country to country. Mince pies or cookies and a glass of milk or sherry are the most common refreshments offered. Some even suggest extra strong mints in case of airsickness.

Once in the house Santa is busy filling the stockings and putting the presents around the tree. He keeps a careful list of what he has given to whom. He warms himself at the fire if there is one, eats and drinks, and then gets on his way because it is a long, long night.

INDEX

PICTURE CREDITS

Bildarchiv Preussischer Kulturbesitz: 102; 106. B & U International Picture Service: 28 T, B; 103; 104 B. The Coca-Cola Company: 60; 61 L, R. Hulton Deutsch Collection: 23 R; 83; 84; 85; 86; 87; 88. The Image Bank: 7; 14 T, B; 15 L, R; 48; 104 T; 124 R. Kurt S. Adler, Inc.: 105 T, B; 122 L, R; 125. Library of Congress: 19; 24; 25; 26; 27; 29; 35; 36; 37; 39 L; 40; 43 L; 47 L; 49 L; 50 R; 52 R; 65; 66; 67; 70 L, R; 73 L, R; 77 R; 120. Leberl Group/Fortnum & Mason: 13. Mansell Collection: 93; 94 L. Stockphotos: 16. The publisher also thanks especially John DeMarco for supplying many of the cards, magazines and suchlike that illustrate this book.